WOMEN'S ISSUES

BY JESSICA MORRISON

Weigl

Published by Weigl Educational Publishers Limited
6325 10th Street SE
Calgary, Alberta, Canada
T2H 2Z9

Website: www.weigl.com

Library and Archives Canada Cataloguing in Publication data available upon request.
Fax (403) 233-7769 for the attention of the Publishing Records department.

ISBN 978-1-55388-689-1 (hard cover)
ISBN 978-1-55388-694-5 (soft cover)

Printed in the United States of America in North Mankato, Minnesota
1 2 3 4 5 6 7 8 9 0 14 13 12 11 10

072010
WEP230610

All of the Internet URLs given in the book were valid at the time of publication. However, due to the dynamic nature of the Internet, some addresses may have changed, or sites may have ceased to exist since publication. While the author and publisher regret any inconvenience this may cause readers, no responsibility for any such changes can be accepted by either the author or the publisher.

Weigl acknowledges Getty Images, Library and Archives Canada, Glenbow Museum, Alamy, and Roberta Bondar as image suppliers for this title.

Every reasonable effort has been made to trace ownership and to obtain permission to reprint copyright material. The publishers would be pleased to have any errors or omissions brought to their attention so that they may be corrected in subsequent printings.

We acknowledge the financial support of the Government of Canada through the Canada Book Fund for our publishing activities.

EDITOR: Heather Kissock
DESIGN: Terry Paulhus

Women's Issues Through The Years

Canada is known throughout the world as a country that accepts and appreciates diversity. People of different ethnic backgrounds, faiths, beliefs, and genders often come to Canada because they believe that they will be treated fairly and be on equal ground with other Canadian citizens. For the most part, Canada's laws have been developed to ensure that this equal treatment occurs.

This was not always the case, however. In fact, for years, certain **demographic** groups were denied the rights that other Canadians had. One group that was affected by unfair laws was the country's women. For a long time, women were not mentioned in the country's **Constitution**. This meant that they were not considered to be Canadian citizens. As a result, their lives were not protected in the same way as many men.

4

When women are not given the same rights as men, it is known as gender discrimination. Discrimination is the unfair treatment of people because of their differences. In the past, women were treated as non-citizens because of the belief that they were the "weaker sex." They were property of their families until they married. Then, they became the property of their husbands. Women had few rights of their own because they were not seen as independent individuals.

Over the years, many Canadian women have fought to develop a new identity that would see them treated as equals alongside men. This movement toward women's rights has drastically changed the way women are viewed and treated in this country. There is, however, still work to be done. Today, Canada's women continue to campaign for their rights and the rights of women around the world.

**Status of Women in
Canada in Decline**

2010

Status of Women in
Canada in Decline

A report released by the Canadian
Feminist Alliance for
International Action and the
Canadian Labour Congress
indicated that the status of women
in Canada has been in gradual
decline since 2004. The decline
was attributed to the withdrawal
of funding for women's **advocacy**
groups, the closure of 12 out of
16 offices that handled women's
rights issues, the elimination of
the country's national childcare
program, and the widening wage
gap between men and women. In
2001, men made about 18 percent
more in earnings than women.
This gap is about six percent
higher than it was 10 years before.

2001

Female soldiers are allowed
to serve in submarines.

2002

Women make up about
one third of the Senate.

2003

Astronaut Roberta Bondar is
named one of *TIME* magazine's
five top Canadian explorers.

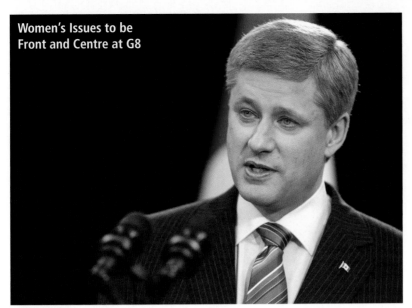

Women's Issues to be Front and Centre at G8

2010

Women's Issues Front and Centre at G8

As host of the 2010 G8 conference, a meeting of the leaders of the top eight industrialized countries, Prime Minister Stephen Harper announced that women's issues would be the key topic of discussion. Specifically, the leaders would be challenged to find solutions to the growing problem of maternal and child **mortality** rates in developing countries. In his announcement, Harper drew attention to the fact that almost 500,000 women in developing countries die in childbirth each year. About nine million children in these areas do not live past the age of five. The goal of the conference was to plan initiatives to improve the health and living conditions of women and children living in the world's developing countries.

2007

Oxfam Canada

In 2007, Oxfam Canada released the Oxfam Canada Strategic Plan. "Walking the Talk on Women's Rights" was a plan to promote changes in policy and actions toward women's rights over the course of six years. The plan focussed on **equality** between men and women in many areas of society. Oxfam began working overseas, in Canada, and around the world to build relationships between women, leaders, and citizens. The ultimate goals were to provide women worldwide with access to resources and legislation that will empower them and promote active citizenship. This plan is still in operation today.

Oxfam Canada

2004

The 75th Anniversary of the Persons' Case is celebrated.

2005

Male university professors make an average of $17,575 more than their female colleagues.

Canada Supports Women in Southeast Asia

2006

Bev Busson becomes the first female Commissioner of the Royal Canadian Mounted Police.

2007

Oxfam releases the Oxfam Canada Strategic Plan, a six-year plan to focus on women's rights.

Canada Ratifies UN Protocol

Canada Ratifies UN Protocol

In October, Canada ratified the United Nations' Convention on the Elimination of All Forms of Discrimination against Women (CEDAW). In doing this, it agreed to the policies and practices by which the United Nations expects women to be treated. CEDAW was established in 1979 and is often called the International Bill of Rights for Women. The convention provides the basis for realizing equality between women and men. By agreeing to the convention's terms, countries are responsible for ensuring women's equal access to, and equal opportunities in, political and public life, as well as education, employment, family law, child care, and social security.

2003

Canada Supports Women in Southeast Asia

The Canadian government committed $6.6 million to the United Nations Development Fund for Women (UNIFEM) to promote and protect women's rights in seven Southeast Asian countries. The money came from the Canadian International Development Agency, a government organization that helps developing countries.

It helped the governments and social agencies of these countries adopt the policies laid out in the United Nations' Convention on the Elimination of All Forms of Discrimination against Women (CEDAW). This document outlines the acts that constitute discrimination and the action plan to eliminate them. This funding was the largest commitment to date for the implementation of CEDAW by any country.

Into the Future

Gender issues are constantly changing and shifting as time goes by. What are some of the issues that people of different genders face today? How do you think they compare to the issues faced 100 years ago? Do you believe that men and women are treated as equals? What can you do today to raise awareness of these issues?

2008

About 22 percent of winning candidates in the 2008 federal election are female.

2009

There are 821,000 self-employed women.

Women in Canadian Hockey

1990

Women in Canadian Hockey

In 1990, the first Women's World Ice Hockey Championship was held in Ottawa, Ontario. Eight teams competed to be named best in the world. Ultimately, the Canadian women's hockey team won the championship, beating the United States 5–2. This feat was quickly followed by other advances in women's hockey. Two years later, Manon Rheaume became the first professional female hockey player in the National Hockey League. She was a goalie for the Tampa Bay Lightning and played in some pre-season games. In 1998, women's hockey became an official event at the Olympics. That year, the Canadian women's hockey team won the silver medal at the Winter Olympics in Nagano, Japan.

1991

Rita Johnston of British Columbia becomes the first woman to serve as a provincial premier.

1992

Canada declares October to be Women's History Month.

National Day of Mourning

1991

National Day of Mourning

Canada's Parliament declared December 6 the National Day of Mourning and Action on Violence against Women. The day was set aside to remember these women and to reflect on the violence women experience in society. The day coincides with the anniversary of the Montreal Massacre of 1989. On this date, a man entered l'École Polytechnique de Montréal and fatally shot 14 women. He killed them because they were women.

1992

Aboriginal Women and Canada's Constitution

In 1992, the federal government began the process of updating and revising Canada's Constitution. During the Constitution talks of 1992, the government made serious efforts to gain the Aboriginal perspective so that Canada's Aboriginal Peoples would be treated fairly and with respect. However, the Native Women's Association of Canada (NWAC), which represented the voice of Canada's Aboriginal women, was left out of the discussions. The NWAC challenged this exclusion by taking the issue to the Supreme Court of Canada. They claimed that their right to equality and freedom of expression under Canada's Charter of Rights and Freedoms was being violated. The Supreme court rejected their case, stating that the federal government had the right to decide the participants in their discussions.

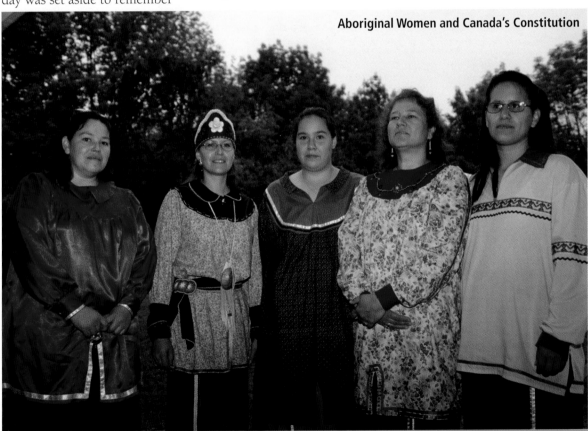
Aboriginal Women and Canada's Constitution

1993

Kim Campbell becomes the first female prime minister of Canada.

1994

Carol Shields wins the Pulitzer Prize for her novel *The Stone Diaries*.

1995

The United Nations holds its fourth conference on women.

1992

Women in Space

From a young age, Roberta Bondar was fascinated with science and science fiction. She often imagined herself as a character in Flash Gordon stories, travelling in outer space and contacting beings from other worlds. Bondar's love of science developed into a career in neurobiology. Her love of science fiction led her to become Canada's first female in space. After nine years of astronaut training, she launched into space on board the space shuttle *Discovery* on January 22.

Women in Space

1996

Bev Busson becomes Superintendent of the RCMP.

1997

Emily Stowe, Canada's first female doctor, is named a National Historic Person.

1998

Sandra Schmirler's curling team wins Olympic gold.

The International Women's Rights Project

The International Women's Rights Project

The International Women's Rights Project (IWRP) was founded with the goal of strengthening women's organizations in Canada and around the world so that human rights standards can be put into place internationally. One project at a time, the IWRP works with student interns, volunteers, and associates from other countries.

Its goal is to provide leadership, guidance, and knowledge to a number of students from several areas. The IWRP is also actively involved in providing resources for women and young girls in rural areas.

Into the Future

Today, many women are entering the fields of math, science, and engineering. Some are teaching at universities, while others are working in the field, writing books and publishing papers in academic journals. Can you think of any female scientists? Do you think females face different obstacles in these careers?

1999

A monument in honour of the **Famous Five** is unveiled in Calgary, Alberta.

2000

Captain Maryse Carmichael becomes the first female to fly with the Snowbirds.

Women's Issues
1980s

The Charter of Rights
and Freedoms

The Charter of Rights and Freedoms

In 1982, the Canadian Charter of Rights and Freedoms was adopted. The Charter spelled out and guaranteed specific rights to everyone in Canada. Unlike other government documents, the Charter of Rights and Freedoms includes a section about rights that are based on racial and gender equality. As a result of this section of the Charter, the Canadian government stated that every person, no matter their race or gender, would be given the same protection under the law. Discrimination for any reason would be against the law.

The Indian Act Revised

1981	1982	1983
Women **lobby** Parliament to include women's rights in the Constitution.	Marguerite Bourgeoys is the first Canadian woman to be canonized.	Roberta Bondar is chosen to be Canada's first female astronaut.

The Indian Act Revised

The Indian Act was created in 1951 to set standards for the way Canada's First Nations would be treated by the federal government. The act detailed procedures on the management of **reserve** lands, funding, and local government. It also set the rules for defining status Indians. Status Indians are First Nations individuals who are entitled to live on reserve lands and participate in government programs. One of the rules put into the act concerned First Nations women who married non-Aboriginal men. The rule stated that, when this happened, the woman was required by law to give up her Indian status. This created many problems for Canada's First Nations women and their families. In 1985, the Canadian Indian Act was changed, allowing Aboriginal women to keep their Indian status when they married a non-Aboriginal.

1986

Sharon Wood

Sharon Wood was the first North American woman to reach the top of Mount Everest. Wood grew up in Vancouver, British Columbia, but moved to the Canadian Rocky Mountains as a teenager. Here, she began taking courses in mountain climbing and tackling gradually higher peaks. In 1977, Wood climbed Canada's highest peak, Mount Logan. She followed this up with climbs in countries such as Argentina, Peru, and the United States. In 1986, Wood flew to Nepal to tackle Mount Everest. She reached the summit on May 20. Following her climb, she was recognized with the Tenzing Norgay Professional Mountaineer of the Year award. This award is named after the sherpa, or guide, that helped Sir Edmund Hillary become the first person to summit Everest.

Sharon Wood

1984

Jeanne Sauvé is the first woman to be appointed governor general of Canada.

1985

The United Nations holds its third international conference on women's issues.

Project Haven

1989

Project Haven

To meet the needs of women and children escaping from abuse and violence, the Canada Mortgage and Housing Corporation, in co-operation with national and provincial governments, began creating transition homes, or shelters, across the country. Most of these homes were located in remote areas or in places that did not currently have such a facility. The program focussed on women in rural areas, Aboriginal women, immigrant women, and women with disabilities. By 1993, Project Haven had developed 78 new shelters.

1989

Women in Engineering and Science

As part of its efforts to encourage women to enter non-traditional job fields, the National Research Council introduced a program called Women in Engineering and Science (WES). This program provided work placements for women studying science, engineering, or mathematics at the university level. The program matched these students with world-class researchers and facilities. Placements took the form of summer jobs or co-operative training opportunities. As a result of the program, hundreds of female students were able to pursue a career in these fields.

Women in Engineering and Science

1986

Sports Canada issues its Policy on Women.

1987

Geraldine Kenney-Wallace is the first woman chair of the Science Council.

1988

Ethel Blondin becomes the first Aboriginal woman to sit in the House of Commons.

1989

Women and the Modern Military

Prior to 1989, women in Canada's military had been assigned to roles that kept them away from actual combat. Initially, most women who wanted to be in the armed forces joined as nurses. During World War II, women began working as mechanics and parachute riggers. All of these positions were supporting roles to the men who actually fought. The role of women in the Canadian Armed Forces changed in 1989 when the Canadian Armed Forces opened almost all jobs, including combat roles, to women. The only jobs that women could not apply for were on submarines. More than a decade later, submarine jobs would also open up for women.

Into the Future

More than 7,900 women are currently serving in the regular armed forces. Another 4,800 are serving in the primary reserve. In May 2006, the first active combat female was killed during battle in Afghanistan. Captain Nichola Goddard is a symbol of strength and equality for Canadian women. Do you know any women who work in the Canadian military? Are there any women in your family who served in World War II? Have you asked about her experiences? What could you learn from her?

1989

Audrey McLaughlin wins the leadership of the NDP, becoming the first woman to lead a federal political party.

1990

Team Canada wins the first Women's World Hockey Championship.

Women's Issues
1970s

Canadian Women's Liberation Movement

In December 1970, nearly 300 women attended a conference at the University of Saskatchewan. It was the first national conference of the Canadian women's liberation movement. This movement was created to fight for women's rights and gender equality. This was the first time Canadian women had gathered together in a large group to discuss the issues they faced as women. At the conference, the women spoke about women's rights, held debates, and developed ideas and activities to spread awareness of women's issues. In the same year, the first women's studies courses were offered at six major universities in Canada. These courses covered topics such as gender equality, **activism**, and feminism.

Canadian Women's Liberation Movement

1971

Women in the **labour force** earn 58

1972

Muriel McQueen Fergusson becomes the first

1974

Pauline Jewett

Pauline Jewett made major advances in women's rights in the seventies. She served as a member of Parliament from 1963 until 1974. During this time, she became known as an advocate for social justice and women's equality. In 1974, Jewett became the president of Simon Fraser University, in British Columbia. This made her the first female president of a non-religious public university in Canada. One hundred years earlier, women were not even allowed to enrol or graduate from most Canadian universities.

1974

Women and Law Enforcement

In 1873, a central police force was established for Canada. This force became known as the Royal Canadian Mounted Police (RCMP). For 101 years, only men were allowed to join the RCMP. As society grew, so did the need for more police officers. On September 16, 1974, the first women were accepted into the RCMP. There were 32 women in total, and they had to complete five months of training in Regina, Saskatchewan. The women joining the RCMP had to complete the same physical requirements as men. Upon graduation, these women would be given the same types of jobs as men, such as highway patrol and criminal and drug investigation. Today, women make up about one-sixth of the Canadian police forces.

Women and Law Enforcement

Pauline Jewett

1973
Sylvia Fedoruk is the first

1974
The first National Conference

1975
The United Nations declares 1975

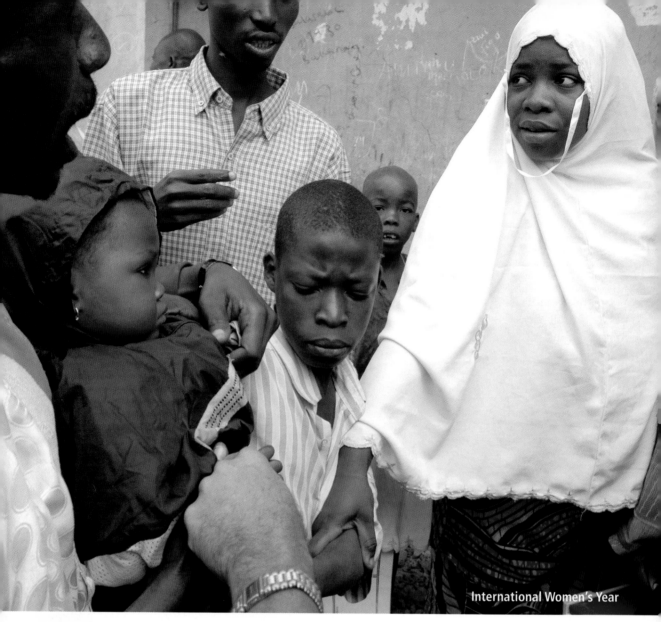

International Women's Year

1975

International Women's Year

The United Nations declared 1975 to be International Women's Year. It did this to draw attention to women's issues and promote advocacy. Many programs were started because of increased awareness, including the United Nations Development Fund for Women (UNIFEM) and the International Women's Tribune Centre, which provides programs to low-income women in developing countries. Since 1975, March 8 has been named International Women's Day. This is a day to celebrate the achievements of women in different areas of society. International Women's Day continues to be celebrated all over the world. In Canada, International Women's Day has become a week-long event, with many activities across the country. Every year, a new theme is chosen for the event.

1976

Iona Campagnolo becomes Canada's first Minister of Sport.

1977

The Canadian Human Rights Act is enacted to stop discrimination

1978

It becomes illegal for women to be fired for becoming pregnant.

Take Back the Night

1978

Take Back the Night

Vancouver was the first Canadian city to hold a Take Back the Night march. These marches are held all over the world. Their goal is to increase awareness about violence towards women.

Only women march in Take Back the Night. This is to demonstrate that women are determined to walk the streets by themselves without fear. The march signifies issues such as safety, **empowerment**, and strength

for women. Today, Take Back the Night marches are held across the country on the third Friday in September.

Into the Future

International Women's Day has been celebrated for many years. Does your school participate in this special day? What are some activities you could organize that would help raise awareness about this day? If you were in charge of organizing the theme for International Women's Day this year, what theme would you choose? How would you promote the day?

1979

Female students enrol in Canadian

1980

The first woman to be elected leader of a provincial

Women's Issues
1960s

Women and Education

Women and Education

In 1960, slightly more than 26,000 women attended university for an undergraduate degree. During the same year, more than 80,000 men attended. It was standard to see many more men attend university at this time, as women were often discouraged from attending. Women that could not be trained in school found it difficult to get well-paying jobs. This meant that many women depended on their husbands for money and support. Over the course of the 1960s, more and more women began attending institutions for higher education, such as colleges and universities. By 1970, more than 41,000 Ontario women were attending university. About 80,000 men attended at the same time. Although they were often discriminated against, many women took control of their education and went to school whenever they could.

1961	1962	1963
Poet Pauline Johnson is the first women to appear on a Canadian postage stamp.	Ontario enacts its Human Rights Code.	Ringette, a women's ice sport invented in Canada, is introduced.

Human Rights Code

for many Canadians. It was also the first human rights act that had a full-time staff to ensure it was followed. In the years to come, other provinces in Canada enacted their own similar Human Rights Codes.

1967

The Hart House Protest

In the late 1960s, about 36 percent of students attending university in Canada were female. However, some aspects of university life were still not open to women. At the University of Toronto, all students paid fees toward Hart House, the university cultural and athletic club. Even though all students paid fees, women were told they were not allowed to enter. In 1967, several women protested in front of Hart House. They demanded that the "men-only" policy be thrown out, so that women could also attend. Hart House opened up to women at the university soon after.

1962

Human Rights Code

In 1962, the province of Ontario repealed, or cancelled, most of its old human rights laws as they were perceived to be outdated for the times. The new Ontario Human Rights Code was the first comprehensive human rights code in Canada. It protected different types of people from many forms of discrimination. This code made it illegal to discriminate against people because of their race, colour, ancestry, nationality, and origin. Although the code did not protect people on the basis of their sex or gender, it was still a step forward for human rights and equality. The Human Rights Code of Ontario was the beginning of a shift in thinking

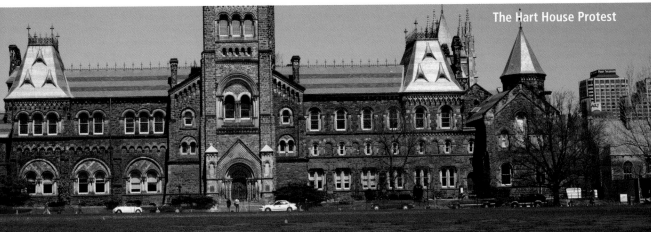
The Hart House Protest

1964

Mary Baker is the first female to become a radio sportscaster in Canada.

1965

The first woman elected to the British Columbia House of Commons is Grace MacInnis.

1967

The Royal Commission on the Status of Women

The gender issues facing women in Canadian society were not easily fixed. It became necessary to observe and document many of the problems women faced. In 1967, the Royal Canadian Commission on the Status of Women was established. This was a group of people that could observe women in society and make suggestions to the government. Their job was to ensure equal opportunities with men in the areas of work, home life, education, and health. The chair of the Commission was Florence Bird. She was also a broadcaster, journalist, and senator. Members of the commission discovered that although eight out of 10 provinces had equal pay laws, women were still paid less for doing the same work. They also found that women made up a small percentage of managers in the workplace. In 1970, the commission wrote a report with 167 recommendations that would give women equal rights.

The Royal Commission on the Status of Women

1966

There are fewer than 900 women in Canada's armed forces.

1967

The United Nations adopts the Declaration of Elimination of Discrimination Against Women.

1968

The Royal Commission on the Status of Women begins.

The Women's Movement

By the late 1960s, women had been working hard to establish their rights and equality in society. There had been several steps forward. However, there were still many areas where women were discriminated against and treated poorly. Women all across Canada wanted more change. As a result, a new movement began. From Vancouver to St. John's, hundreds of women formed groups. Their goal was to advocate women's rights. These groups did not believe that small changes were enough. In Vancouver, the Women's Caucus was established. In Montreal, the Women's Liberation Movement soon followed. All of these groups raised awareness of women's issues. Others provided services such as daycare, shelters for women affected by violence, and health centres. Most

The Women's Movement

organizations in the Women's Movement made publications, such as flyers, posters, manuals, and books for distribution to the general public. This helped to create a network of advocates. By the end of the decade, the women's movement was providing a powerful voice for Canadian women.

Into the Future

You have probably heard of the Women's Movement before. What do the words "liberation" and "equality" mean to you? Are there places where you do not feel that women are treated as equals? What could you do to change this?

1969

About 36 percent of university undergraduate students are women.

1970

The first women's studies courses are offered at Canadian universities.

Fair Employment Practices Act in Ontario

1951

Fair Employment Practices Act in Ontario

As with other provinces in Canada, Ontario women suffered from many discriminatory acts at work. They were often not paid as much as men in their field and were restricted from doing certain jobs. Typically, women were expected to do household tasks, cooking, secretarial work, teaching, and nursing. However, on April 5, Ontario made a step in the direction of equality. The Female Employee's Fair **Remuneration** Act and the Fair Employment Act were both enacted. These laws targeted discrimination in work environments and in hiring practices. They also established a complaint procedure for people who were being mistreated at work. The Female Employee's Fair Remuneration Act protected women from being placed in lower paying jobs simply because of their gender. It ensured that women workers of Ontario would receive equal pay for work of equal value. Later, this law would be enacted federally.

1951

The Canadian military begins to recruit women.

1952

Elsie Knott, from Curve Lake First Nation in Ontario, is the first woman to be elected chief of a nation.

1953

The first women serve on a jury in Canada.

1954

Women's Bureau of Labour

With more and more women taking jobs outside the home, it became necessary to start an organization to oversee the changes in the workforce. The Women's Bureau of Labour was created by the Department of Labour and the National Council of Women in Canada in 1954. This was a federal government unit that provided leadership and services to women in the workforce. The bureau planned and promoted policies and programs that helped women achieve equality in the workplace, from job opportunities and pay to rights and benefits. It also provided educational opportunities for working women and those wanting to enter the workforce.

1955

A Part of the Team

Eight-year-old Abby Hoffman wanted to play hockey with the boys. She cut her hair, donned her jersey, and hit the ice as a defence player. No one even knew she was a girl. She played for much of the season until it was time for the all-star game. In order to participate, Hoffman had to supply the organizers with her birth certificate. When they learned she was a girl, Hoffman was dismissed from the team. She was no longer allowed to play hockey, but she started a trend. Young girls across Canada started trying out for boys' hockey teams.

A Part of the Team

1954

Marilyn Bell is the first person to swim across Lake Ontario.

1955

A new Canadian law states that women can no longer be fired from federal public service jobs when they get married.

Ellen Louks Fairclough

Ellen Louks Fairclough was born in Hamilton, Ontario, in 1905. In 1950, she was elected to the Canadian House of Commons. During her time in office, Fairclough made more than 150 speeches per year, many focussing on the status of women in society. She also introduced many bills for equal pay and was a staunch advocate of women's rights. After the 1957 federal election, Prime Minister John Diefenbaker appointed Fairclough to the Cabinet as Secretary of State for Canada. Fairclough became the first woman to serve as a member of the Canadian Cabinet. She later acted as the Minister of Citizenship and Immigration and Postmaster General. In both 1957 and 1958, Ellen Fairclough was named Woman of the Year by journalists. The Province of Ontario named her Outstanding Woman for all of her work. In 2005, Canada Post issued a postage stamp in her honour.

Ellen Louks Fairclough

1956

The federal government passes the Female Employees Equal Pay Act.

1957

Ellen Fairclough is the first woman to be appointed to the federal Cabinet.

1958

Blanche Margaret Meagher is named the ambassador to Israel.

1959

The National Ballet School

The late 1950s saw several changes in media and recreation. Women were expressing themselves in many ways, including song, theatre, and dance. In 1959, Betty Oliphant and Celia Franca opened the National Ballet School in Toronto. This was a place where women and men could study dance and expression, without being discriminated against. Their first enrolment was 27 female students. Afterschool programs also ran for 202 students, nine of whom were boys.

The National Ballet School

Into the Future

In the past, many people believed that certain activities were gender specific. This means that only men or women should take part in them. Activities such as dancing, singing, and housework were often seen as "womanly." Working with machinery and other forms of physical labour were often seen as men's work. This type of thinking is called stereotyping. Do you think people discriminate against others today based on the activities they choose to do? What can you do to change this?

1959

Marie-Marguerite d'Youville is the first Canadian-born candidate for sainthood.

1960

The Canadian Bill of Rights is passed.

Women's Issues
1940s

Suffragists in Quebec

1941	**1942**	**1943**
Women are allowed to enlist in the Canadian Army.	The Women's Royal Canadian Naval Service is established.	Many women join the labour force, filling positions left by men who went to war.

1940s

Suffragists in Quebec

By 1940, all of Canada's provinces, except Quebec, had made it legal for women to vote and run for office. However, after pressure from **suffragists**, Quebec finally signed the Act Granting Women the Right to Vote and to be Eligible as Candidates. This occurred on April 25 and marked a very special day for women's rights advocates living in the province. Soon after, the women of Quebec were also given the right to practise law.

1939–1945

Women at War

When World War II began, Canadian women once again signed up to help the war effort. Initially, most served as nurses, working in hospitals and casualty stations overseas. As in World War I, women were still not allowed to participate in combat roles. However, in 1941, the military made changes to broaden the roles women could assume in the forces. That year, they decided to enlist 45,000 women in roles beyond nursing. All three arms of the military—the army, the navy, and the air force—created women's divisions. The air force was the first to do this, creating the Canadian Women's Auxiliary Air Force. The Canadian Women's Army Corps (CWACs) and the Women's Royal Canadian Naval Services (WRENs) soon followed. Within their divisions, women took on jobs ranging from cooks and clerical workers to mechanics and heavy equipment operators. While these women did not engage in combat, they were sent overseas to provide support to the men who did.

1944

Women's Health Issues

In 1944, the Victorian Order of Nurses and several public health departments began to offer prenatal courses for pregnant women. These pregnancy and childbirth classes helped women through the physical aspects of birth as well as the emotional and familial issues of having a child. Previously, many women did not have help with some of these issues. Soon after the start of these classes, the government began to offer baby bonuses and pay allowances for young families. This additional money helped families cope with the costs of an increased family size.

Women at War

Women's Health Issues

1944

The federal government passes the Family Allowance Act, providing financial support to young families.

1945

World War II officially ends. Thousands of women have served overseas and at home.

Equal Pay for Female Teachers

1946

Viola Desmond, a black woman, is arrested for sitting in the white section of a Nova Scotia theatre.

1947

The government declares that women will not lose their Canadian citizenship if they marry a non-Canadian.

1946

Equal Pay for Female Teachers

Teaching and nursing were common jobs for women in the mid-1900s. However, men and women doing the same job did not receive the same amount of money in return for their work. Women in teaching and other professions were paid much less for their work than men. Unequal pay was a serious issue that women's rights advocates wanted dealt with. In 1946, the Ontario Teachers Federation approved the principle of equal pay for men and women teachers. Many saw this as a big step forward for Ontario women.

1946

Women's Corps Disbanded

Canadian women played a significant role in World War II. Many were injured, and some were even killed while serving their country. However, when the war ended, the government decided that women were no longer needed in the military as their missions had been completed. In 1946, all three women's divisions were disbanded. In future years, however, the role of women in World War II would be remembered and would allow for women to become part of the regular forces, fighting alongside the men.

Women's Corps Disbanded

Into the Future

The armed forces was one of the first organizations to begin treating women on an equal basis with men. The process, however, was slow and came in spurts directly related to war. Still, over time, women have achieved equality in the military and in other areas as well. Can you think of any jobs that are still inaccessible to women? Why do you think this is? What do you think will be needed to instigate change in this area?

1948

The United Nations enacts the Universal Declaration of Human Rights.

1949

Cairine Wilson becomes Canada's first female delegate to the UN.

1950

Marion Orr becomes the first woman in Canada to open a flying school.

1930s

Queen of the Hurricanes

Elsie MacGill was a true pioneer in the women's movement. By the 1930s, she had become the first Canadian woman to earn a degree in electrical engineering and the first woman in North America to earn an aeronautical engineering degree. With these credentials in hand, she took a job as chief aeronautical engineer with Canadian Car and Foundry. Here, she began to design and supervise the construction of airplanes. One of the airplanes she was responsible for was the Hawker Hurricane. This was a fighter plane built for both the Canadian and British Air Force to use during the war. By the end of the war, MacGill had supervised the construction of about 1,450 of these airplanes. Following the war, she became involved in promoting women's issues, such as daycare and maternity leave. MacGill's influence was so respected that she was appointed to the Royal Commission on the Status of Women in 1967. As part of the commission, she met with women across the country to discuss their views on gender equality. The results of these discussions were used to suggest new government policies in relation to the treatment of women in society.

Queen of the Hurricanes

1931	1932	1933
Louise McKinney, a member of the **Famous Five**, dies at the age of 63.	Dr. Elizabeth Bagshaw opens the first family planning clinic in Canada.	Emily Murphy, one of the Famous Five, dies at the age of 65.

Women in Law and Legislature

By the mid-1930s, some women in Canada had gained the right to vote. Others, however, were still fighting for this right.

In 1934, the women of New Brunswick won the right to hold provincial office. This meant they were allowed to run in an election, along with men. Women were slowly making their way into many areas of law and legislature. In 1935, Helen Alice Kinnear became the first woman lawyer in Canada to stand in front of the Supreme Court of Canada. A year later, Barbara Hanley was elected as mayor of the town of Webwood, Ontario. She was the first female mayor in the country.

Women in Law and Legislature

1934

New Brunswick women win the right to hold provincial office.

1935

Helen Alice Kinnear is the first female lawyer to appear before the Supreme Court of Canada.

Lea Roback

Lea Roback

In the 1930s, many parents needed to work for 60 or more hours every week to provide for their families. Lea Roback was a social activist and advocate for equality and women's rights. In 1937, she led 5,000 employees working in the garment industry on a strike. For 25 days, the employees protested 60 hour work weeks, terrible working conditions, and low wages. This action and similar events led to a revision of the minimum wage laws a year later.

Volunteering for War

G 149-5-20

1938

Volunteering for War

In 1938, it was becoming apparent that international tensions were leading to war. As in World War I, women wanted to play a role, but they still were not allowed to join the military in any capacity beyond nursing. Many women did not have nursing training, but they wanted to contribute. In 1938, a group of women in British Columbia became the first to form a volunteer organization to provide support to the military. Called the British Columbia Women's Service Corps, they trained in first aid, mechanics, and clerical work. Within months of the declaration of war, similar groups had popped up across the country. Their training took on a military slant, with many women learning how to signal codes and read maps. As they became more qualified to be military personnel, they began to lobby the government to remove them from volunteer status and make them full-time members of the regular forces. The government had to weigh its need for military workers against society's traditional view of women's roles. Over time, women were allowed to participate more fully in the military.

1936

Barbara Hanley becomes the first woman mayor of a Canadian town.

1937

Lea Roback leads 5,000 Montreal garment workers in a strike.

A Girl Called Intrepid

1939

A Girl Called Intrepid

At the beginning of the war, Kay Martin was attending college in Boston, Massachusetts. One day, on a visit home to New Brunswick, she was taken to a museum basement and told that she was about to serve her country for the war effort. She was to courier secret documents between the United States and Great Britain. Many of these documents reported on enemy movement and planned attacks, including the bombing of Pearl Harbor. Shortly after Pearl Harbor, she was ordered back to New Brunswick, only two months before graduating. Back in Canada, she began working for the military. On the surface, she was a secretary, but behind the scenes, she was actually an intelligence officer who broke enemy codes. She performed this role until the end of the war. Her services no longer required, she returned to civilian life, married, and had children. No one knew of her secret life until 1976, when her cover was exposed by William Stevenson's book titled *A Man Called Intrepid*, which detailed the entire operation.

Into the Future

In the past, many women were told they were not able to do the types of jobs they wanted to do because they were not skilled or they were not suited well for them. What are some of your skills? Make a list of activities you enjoy doing. What types of jobs do you think are well suited to your skills? How do you think people would have responded to you in the 1930s if you wanted to use your skills for a certain job?

1938

All provinces except Nova Scotia amend their minimum wage law to apply to both men and women.

1939

Elsie MacGill is the first female engineer to design an airplane.

1940

Quebec women win the right to vote and run for office.

Women's Issues
1920s

Maternity Leave

1921
Agnes Macphail becomes the first woman to sit in Parliament.

1922
The women of Prince Edward Island win the right to vote.

1923
Bertha Wilson, Canada's first female Supreme Court judge, is born.

The Federal Divorce Law

1921

Maternity Leave

As more women began to enter the work force, it became necessary to examine the unique needs they had as workers. One issue was the treatment of women who were pregnant or recent mothers. In 1921, British Columbia became the first province to draw up a labour law relating to new mothers. The Maternity Protection Act stated that an employer could not employ a woman until at least six weeks after she had given birth. While basic, for years, this was the only law relating to maternity in Canada. In 1966, British Columbia again led the way by revising the act so that it was less about the employer and more about the woman. Under the revised act, women became entitled to maternity leave. By 1988, all provinces had some kind of legislation regarding maternity rights.

1925

The Federal Divorce Law

Divorce was not common in Canada in the early 20th century. In fact, in many Canadian provinces, it was illegal. However, in 1925, the responsibility for handling divorce was taken from the provinces and put under federal jurisdiction. The federal government developed a law that defined the conditions under which a divorce could be sought. What was unique about the Divorce Law of 1925 was that it applied to both men and women. Prior to 1925, women could only apply for a divorce under special conditions. Now, they could apply for a divorce on the same grounds as men. The fact that women and men were guided by the same conditions under the law was seen as a step forward in the women's rights movement.

1924

Phyllis Munday and Annette Buck are the first women to climb Mount Robson, the highest peak in the Canadian Rockies.

1925

The women of Newfoundland earn the right to vote.

Nellie McClung

Nellie McClung

Nellie McClung was born in Ontario in 1873. At the age of 16, McClung became a teacher for a small school in Manitoba. She was always outspoken and stood up for the rights of older people, mothers, widows, and factory workers. As McClung grew older, she became interested in equality and **social reform**. She was concerned about women, particularly their right to vote and the conditions they worked under. In 1921, McClung was elected into Alberta's Legislative Assembly. While she served, she fought for social equality as well as many other women's issues. She later moved to Alberta and became one of the Famous Five, fighting for the right to have women known as "persons" under the law.

The Persons Case

By the late 1920s, women were slowly achieving rights independent of their husbands and families. Most women in Canada now had the right to vote in elections. Even with this right, however, they still were not considered persons under the law. At the time, Canada functioned under the **British North America Act**. In the act, a group of people were referred to as "persons," and an individual was called "he." No reference was made to women. As a result, women held no legal position in Canada. Therefore, they had no rights or privileges under the law. In 1928, a group of women's rights activists from Alberta decided to take this issue to the Supreme Court of Canada. Nellie McClung, Irene Parlby, Louise McKinney, Henrietta Muir Edwards, and Emily Murphy asked the court if the word "persons" applied to both men and women. The Supreme Court debated the issue and ruled that women were not considered persons under the act. In their decision, the court explained that the BNA Act was written in the 1800s, when women did not have the rights they had now. However, the court also said that there was no **precedent** in Canada or England to justify changing the law. The women decided to take their case to the British Privy Council, the highest court of appeal for Canadians at the time. The Privy Council ruled that the BNA Act was outdated in the way it defined "persons." As a result, women became known as persons under the law and were able to take advantage of the rights and privileges of being persons. Following this victory, the women who had fought for this right became known as the Famous Five.

The Persons Case

1926

The first female Amateur Athletic Foundation is established.

1927

The Famous Five petition the Supreme Court to decide whether the word 'person' in the British North America Act includes women.

1928

Canadian Women in the Olympics

The 1928 Summer Olympic Games in Amsterdam were special for both Canadian women and women in general. These were the first Olympic games that allowed women to participate in track and field events. This was also the first time that Canada sent women team members to the Olympics. Although there were only seven women on the 71-member team, the women won more than 25 percent of Canada's medal count. Canadian women won four medals in total. Saskatchewan's Ethel Catherwood won a gold medal in the women's high jump event. Fanny Rosenfeld of Ontario took the silver in the 100-metre race, and Ethel Stewart won the bronze in the same event. The women's relay team, consisting of Myrtle McGowan, Fanny Rosenfeld, Ethel Stewart, and Florence Doane, won the gold medal in the 400-metre race. Their gold-medal run also set a new world record for that distance.

Into the Future

Before 1929, Canadian law did not acknowledge that women were persons. The Famous Five changed the law by taking a stand and going to court over the issue. Are there any ways that you feel people are being treated unfairly? What are some proactive ways to change their situation?

1928	1929	1930
The Supreme Court denies that women are persons under the law.	The British Privy Council decides that Canadian women are persons under the law.	Cairine Reay Wilson is the first woman appointed to the Senate in Canada.

Women's Issues
1910s

United Farmers and Farm Women of Alberta

Girl Guides of Canada

Girl Guides of Canada

In the early 1900s, a British man named Robert Baden-Powell created a club for boys called the Boy Scouts. Members of the club received training in a range of skills such as map reading and first aid. The scouting program quickly gained popularity in Great Britain and around the world. In 1909, more than 10,000 boys gathered at a scouting rally held in London, England. People were surprised to see that many girls also came. Baden-Powell was impressed. He decided to create a club for girls as well. The club became

known as the Girl Guides. By 1910, a Girl Guides program was in place in St. Catharines, Ontario. Within two years, there were Girl Guide programs in every province of Canada. By 1917, the Canadian Girl Guides Association had been formed. This association helped plan programming for the Girl Guides. The programs were designed to prepare young girls for the challenges they would meet in life. Some of these challenges changed to suit the times. During World War II, young girls were taught how to change dressings on injured soldiers. Today, many Girl Guides work on anti-bullying campaigns.

Agriculture has always been an important part of Canadian culture. In the early 1900s, farming was a way of life for many Canadians. These people had farms and were earning a living off their land. In 1909, farmers living in Alberta created a group to improve conditions for farmers and other agricultural workers. The group was called the United Farmers Association (UFA). In 1915, the United Farm Women of Alberta was formed as an auxiliary to the UFA. Founded by Irene Parlby, one of the Famous Five, this organization helped educate women about the issues facing them, such as their property rights as farm women and their legal status within Canadian law.

United Farmers and Farm Women of Alberta

1911

Women in the labour force earn 52.8 percent of men's wages.

1912

The first female lawyer to practise law in British Columbia is Mabel French.

1913

Alys McKey Bryant is the first woman in Canada to fly an airplane.

The Vote for Women in Manitoba

Emily Murphy

Women in World War I

1916

The Vote for Women in Manitoba

Prior to 1916, women had never had the right to vote in Canada. Over time, a suffrage movement began to change the laws toward women voting. Women such as Nellie McClung, Ada Powers, Josephine Dandurand, Elizabeth Smith-Shortt, and Emily Murphy held rallies, where they asked people to sign petitions urging the government to change the laws. Many provincial governments would not listen to these women as they fought for the right to vote. However, in 1916, the government of Manitoba agreed to amend its Election Act so that women over the age of 21 were allowed to vote in that province. Soon after, Saskatchewan and Alberta amended their laws, giving women the right to vote as well.

1916

Emily Murphy

Emily Murphy was an influential person in the fight for women's

rights in Canada. One of her first accomplishments was convincing the Alberta government to pass the Dower Act in 1911. This act ensured that a woman had a right to a portion of her husband's property. Following this victory, Murphy asked Alberta's attorney general to consider hiring female judges to handle women's court cases. The attorney general agreed with Murphy and, in 1916, appointed her the first female **magistrate** in the **British Empire**. However, her right to become a judge was challenged under the BNA Act's definition of "persons." This challenge led to the Persons Case of 1928.

1917

Women in World War I

Women played an integral part of wartime support. Some women worked directly in the war as nurses, while others took over men's jobs to help the war effort. In 1917, more than 35,000 women worked in factories making munitions. In the same year, Alberta became the first province to declare a

minimum wage law for women working in many of these factories.

1919

The Canadian Federation of University Women

By the late 1910s, most of Canada's larger universities had groups that represented the rights of women on campus. In 1919, representatives from these groups met in Winnipeg to form a national organization. The Canadian Federation of University Women was founded to help improve human rights, peace, justice, education, and the legal status of women. The federation remains in operation today, with more than 10,000 members, belonging to 112 different clubs.

The Canadian Federation of University Women

1914

Canadian nurses begin heading overseas to serve in World War I.

1917

Women in Ontario win the right to vote and hold public office.

Women's Issues
1900s

The Married Women's Property Act

1900

The Married Women's Property Act

When a woman married in the late 1800s, she lost the legal rights to her property. Her husband became the owner of all of her property. In 1900, Manitoba became the first province to reconsider this law. The province introduced its Married Women's Property Act. This law stated that women could buy and sell property and make legal agreements, just like their husbands. In 1903, the province of Prince Edward Island instituted a similar act, and in 1907, Saskatchewan created its own form of the act. These acts gave women the ability to achieve some financial independence separate from their husbands.

The Canadian Women's Suffrage Association

1907

The Canadian Women's Suffrage Association

In the early 1900s, many Canadians did not have the right to vote, run for election, or hold office. Women, along with visible minorities and Aboriginal Peoples, were some of the groups who had few **democratic** rights. Women had been campaigning for voting rights since the late 1800s. Several suffrage organizations had been formed over the years. One of the largest was the Toronto Women's Suffrage Association, which was formed in 1883. In 1907, the group changed its name to the Canadian Suffrage Association in order to broaden its scope nationally. The association lobbied for voting rights as well as other issues relating to women. While the right to vote was not immediately successful, the association was able to convince several Toronto colleges and universities to start accepting women as students.

1900

The only type of work that provides

1901

Women make up about 13 percent of

1909

The Criminal Code

Women did not have many of the same protective rights as men in the early 1900s. Before 1909, people who stole livestock would receive harsher punishment than those who kidnapped young women. In 1909, the Criminal Code of Canada declared that it was illegal to abduct women. Before this, it was not illegal to abduct any woman over the age of 16.

The Criminal Code

1909

The Ladies' Reading Room

The Ladies' Reading Room

In 1909, it was unheard of for women to have a special place to discuss issues with other women. The Ladies' Reading Room was one of the first open places where women could hold debates, discuss issues, and hear lectures about women's rights. The Ladies' Reading Room was created after a group of women were banned from attending suffrage debates at a fraternity in St. John's, Newfoundland. A three-dollar membership fee provided women from various backgrounds with a place to meet and discuss suffrage, as well as international and national concerns. Within a few weeks of forming, the club had 125 members.

1903

Emma Baker is the first female to earn her PhD at a Canadian university.

1905

The University of Toronto Medical School allows women students.

1907

The Canadian Suffrage Association is established.

ACTIVITY
Into the Future

Advocates are people who speak for other people. They represent people's issues to governments and other groups that can evoke change. If it were not for advocates, much of the discrimination of the past would still be happening. Gender equality is a constant struggle, yet with advocacy and awareness, progress has been made. One of the main qualities of an advocate is persistence. Many of the men and women in the fight for women's rights faced difficult odds. The Famous Five did not stop their quest for equality. They were advocates for a cause they believed in and helped make changes to society.

Become an Advocate

Over the next week, take note of any issues that you see unfolding in your hometown or other parts of the world. These issues could relate to discrimination, animal welfare, or the environment. Is there any issue that you feel strongly about? Once you have found a cause you care about, try brainstorming ways to bring awareness of the situation to other people. You could organize a speech or rally for your school, or start a blog online. As an advocate, it is important to be respectful of various views while telling people about your cause. Discuss ways that they can help, and listen to their solutions as well. Although it may take time, one person can make big changes in a community and the world.

FURTHER
Research

Many books and websites provide information about women's issues, equality, and rights. To learn more about this topic, borrow books from the library, or surf the Internet.

Books

Most libraries have computers that connect to a database for researching information. If you input a key word, you will be provided with a list of books in the library that contain information on that topic. Non-fiction books are arranged numerically, using their call number. Fiction books are organized alphabetically by the author's last name.

Websites

To learn more about gender issues, equality and women's rights, visit **www.abheritage.ca/famous5**.

For additional information about Canadian women throughout history, visit **www.heroines.ca**.

heroines.ca
A Guide to Women in Canadian History

Home · About · Meet the Author · Contact · People · Gallery · Celebrate · History · Resources · News · Search

Discover some famous Canadian women.

FEATURE VIDEO

Sarah McLachlan singing "I will remember you": PLAY

Meet Canadian astronaut Julie Payette

Canadian hockey star Angela James named to Hockey Hall of Fame

Lilith Fair in Vancouver

Mary McLean oldest lawyer in Canada?

How we remember heroes and heroines
Read Merna Forster's commentary in the Times Colonist

Check out This Month in Canadian Herstory

FEATURE WEBSITES
The Right Honourable Kim Campbell, Canada's 19th Prime Minister
Kootenay Feminism, A Digital Timeline c 2nd Wave Feminism in the West Kootena

People
We Can Do It!
·Heroines
·Biographies
·Group Histories

Gallery
·Pictures
·Cartoons
·Posters

Celebrate
·Stamps
·Statues
·Currency
·Historic Sites
·Women's
  History Month

History
·Time Travel
·This Month in
  Herstory

Resources
Daring Lady Flyers
·Books
·Shop
·Recipes
·Quotes
·Classroom

News
·Upcoming
·Latest News
·Archives

Glossary

activism: taking action to create social change

advocacy: active support of a cause

British Empire: the lands formerly under the rule of Great Britain

British North America Act: a document that serves as the base of Canada's Constitution and sets out the rules of government

Constitution: a set of regulations that helps govern a country

democratic: based on the concept that government is run by the people

demographic: dealing with statistics of age, gender, and income

empowerment: the giving of power or authority

equality: being the same as another; in the case of gender issues, equality means that everyone has the same rights

Famous Five: a group of Alberta women who fought for women's rights

feminist: someone who supports equal rights for women

labour force: people who work for pay

lobby: to attempt to influence government policy

magistrate: a government official assigned to hear and decide cases in court

mortality: loss of life

precedent: a legal case that serves as an example for a later case

remuneration: pay for work

reserve: land set aside for Canada's First Nations

social reform: making changes to society and the way it functions

suffragists: people advocating for women's right to vote

Index